# IMPOSSIBLE SCIENCE

by James Bow

## Crabtree Publishing Company
www.crabtreebooks.com

# Crabtree Publishing Company
## www.crabtreebooks.com

**Author:** James Bow
**Editors:** Molly Aloian, Tim Cooke
**Proofreader:** Kathy Middleton
**Designer:** Lynne Lennon
**Cover Design:** Margaret Amy Salter
**Picture Researcher:** Andrew Webb
**Picture Manager:** Sophie Mortimer
**Art Director:** Jeni Child
**Editorial Director:** Lindsey Lowe
**Children's Publisher:** Anne O'Daly
**Production Coordinator and
   Prepress Technician:** Margaret Amy Salter
**Print Coordinator:** Katherine Berti

**Photographs**
**Cover:** Thinkstock
**Interior: BFI:** 9, 13, 20; **istockphoto:** 27, 28; **Public Domain:** 29; **Shutterstock:** 6, 8, 10, 18–19, 22, 23, 24, 25, Marcel Clemens 5, Nathan B Dappen 12, Ilya Genkin 17, Fer Gregory 4, Zoran Vukma Simokov 26, Darren Whitt 16; **The Kobal Collecion:** Paramount Television 19; **Thinkstock:** Hemera 15, istockphoto 14, Photodisc 21, Photos.com 11; **Topfoto:** Topham Picturepoint 7.

**Library and Archives Canada Cataloguing in Publication**

Bow, James, 1972-
      Impossible science / James Bow.

(Mystery files)
Includes index.
Issued also in electronic formats.
ISBN 978-0-7787-8009-0 (bound).--ISBN 978-0-7787-8014-4 (pbk.)

      1. Science--Juvenile literature. 2. Discoveries in science--Juvenile literature. I. Title. II. Series: Mystery files (St. Catharines, Ont.)

Q163.B69 2012          j500          C2012-906832-2

**Library of Congress Cataloging-in-Publication Data**

CIP available at Library of Congress

## Crabtree Publishing Company
www.crabtreebooks.com          1-800-387-7650

**Published in Canada
Crabtree Publishing**
616 Welland Ave.
St. Catharines, ON
L2M 5V6

**Published in the United States
Crabtree Publishing**
PMB 59051
350 Fifth Avenue, 59th Floor
New York, New York 10118

**Published by CRABTREE PUBLISHING COMPANY in 2013**
Copyright © 2013 Brown Bear Books Ltd

Printed in the U.S.A./112012/FA20121012

# Contents

# Introduction

Scientists make new discoveries every single day. New breakthroughs mean that scientists can achieve things that were impossible only a few years ago. But which scientific ideas are possible and which remain beyond human capability? Imagine a world where you can step inside a booth and transport yourself to the other side of the planet. Imagine smart robots helping you. Imagine a life where people do not get sick and live far longer than we do now.

Imagination has pushed our world forward in ways many of us would not have thought possible a short time ago. Scientists often use the imagination as a starting point.

Are wormholes ways for us to travel into the future?

For centuries, **philosophers**, storytellers, and writers have imagined new technologies or new ways of living. Scientists have explored these ideas and helped make some of them a reality.

## Exploring Ideas

This book explores the impossible ideas and dreams that science has somehow made possible. Even if scientists didn't end up with what they first imagined, exploring these ideas led to other ideas that changed life in big ways.

Mystery words...

philosophers: people who study the nature of reality

# Eternal LIFE

Do you want to live forever? Qin Shi Huangdi
did. In the third century **B.C.E.**, the first
emperor of China ordered his doctors to
create pills that could keep him alive forever.
They made the pills from the chemical mercury,
which is poisonous. It killed the emperor slowly.

Many people have dreamed of eternal life. Spanish explorers in North America first visited Florida to look for a magic fountain, for example. It was said that anyone who drank its waters would live forever. But no such fountain exists—and no one has ever managed to cheat death. The oldest age ever recorded for a human is around 122 years.

## Managing Cells

Living things grow old when the **cells** inside them stop making new cells and die off. Eventually, the organism also dies. Scientists don't yet know how to stop cells from dying. That means eternal life is still impossible. But scientists believe we are close to finding the **gene** (the code within the cell) that tells cells to stop making new cells. Turning off this gene could slow the aging process—or even stop it altogether!

## Mystery File:
### CRYONICS

Cryonics uses liquid nitrogen to freeze human bodies. About 250 people around the world have had their bodies frozen after death. They hope they will be preserved until science can figure out how to bring them back to life.

Mystery words...

**cells:** microscopic divisions of living matter within the body

# Creating LIFE

Many people have wondered if it is possible to create life from nothing. In the early 19th century, Mary Shelley wrote a novel in which a scientist named Frankenstein zapped body parts with electricity to bring a creature to life.

Mary Shelley's story might have a little bit of truth in it. Modern scientists have tried to copy the conditions on early Earth. They put **inorganic** materials in a flask and zapped the mixture with electricity. They created amino acids, which are building blocks of life. But that is a lot different from creating living creatures.

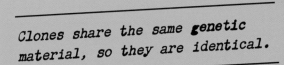

Clones share the same genetic material, so they are identical.

## Life by Cloning

Cloning is one way for scientists to create organisms. Cloning uses cells from a plant or animal to produce an exact copy. The first cloned animal, a sheep named Dolly, was created in 1996. But cloning is not creating life: the cells used are already alive.

Although we can't make new life from nothing, we can change what exists. Genetic engineering lets scientists rewrite cells to change plants and animals. For example, scientists can now make crops resistant to certain diseases, for example.

*Frankenstein used electricity to bring his monster to life.*

Mystery words...

**genetic:** related to genes, which control the growth of the body

# Perpetual MOTION

The scientist Isaac Newton put together the first laws to describe gravity and motion. He said that an object in motion will stay in motion unless it is acted upon by another force. Even before Newton, inventors had looked for a "magic wheel" that would never stop moving— a perpetual motion machine.

Why can't machines work forever?

Such a wheel was tested in Bavaria in the 18th century. Although the wheel rotated for a long time, it always stopped. Rudolph Clausius explained why in 1850 when he wrote the Laws of Thermodynamics. He said that a simple machine

*This machine uses weights to turn a wheel to lift water.*

such as a wheel can't create energy by itself out of nothing. In fact, it will always lose energy.

## Overcoming Friction

The energy in a wheel or any another simple machine is constantly being used up. If machine parts rub together, for example, they lose energy in the form of heat. That is why

### Mystery File:
### USELESS MACHINE?

Even if we eliminated friction, what would a perpetual motion machine do? Once we use it to do something, we take energy away from the machine and slow it down. A perpetual motion machine might be nice, but it is useless.

a rolling ball does not keep on rolling forever. Engineers have reshaped cars and added **lubricants** to machinery to try to reduce **friction**, which slows machinery down. These things help machines go faster for longer or use less energy. But it is impossible to eliminate friction entirely—for now.

Mystery words...

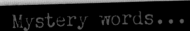

friction: the resistance created when objects rub together

# Time TRAVEL

Would you want to visit the past? We've all seen films in which people use time machines to go backward into the past or forward into the future. It seems like a great idea—but is it possible?

It might be possible. In the early 20th century, Albert Einstein suggested that time is not always the same. It can speed up or slow down. That made scientists wonder when they measured the speed of light if time travel was possible. Nothing moves faster than light, which travels at about 186,000 miles per second (about 300,000 km/s). This means that if people could travel close to the speed of light, time would slow down. An astronaut could travel to the nearest star and back within a single lifetime.

*Einstein claimed time does not always pass at the same speed.*

The astronaut would return to Earth to discover, however, that actually hundreds of years had passed.

## Future Visitors

In theory, being able to move at the speed of light would let us travel into the future. But would we be able to get back? And, if we believe time travel will be possible, why haven't we met people from the future yet?

## Mystery File: QUICKER CLOCKS

Clocks run slower near sources of gravity. The global positioning system (GPS) relies on timing signals bounced to **satellites**. Clocks on satellites run faster than clocks down here due to Earth's gravity. GPS has to correct for the effect.

## Mystery words...

satellites: objects that orbit around a planet.

13

# Faster than LIGHT

Nothing can travel faster than the speed of light.

Space is so big that light takes a full eight minutes to travel from the Sun to Earth. Right now, it would take a space shuttle 165,000 years at full speed to reach our nearest star, Alpha Centauri. **Science fiction** writers did not want to wait that long. They imagined spacecraft that could break the speed of light.

Mystery words...

science fiction: stories based on future technology and science

Nothing travels faster than light, but is it possible to get close to light speed? Space rockets only fire for a few minutes after launch; the rest of the time they use momentum to keep up speed. If a rocket kept firing, would it keep **accelerating**?

## Infinite Energy

A steady acceleration would reach 90 percent of the speed of light in 15 months. The energy needed to do it would be huge, and the need would increase as speed increased. Near the speed of light, the energy required to push us faster increases to infinity—and that amount of energy does not exist.

The closer you came to the speed of light, the slower time would pass for you. If you were going close enough to the speed of light, time would slow down so much that you could **visit** any star in the universe within your own lifetime.

In stories, spacecraft can travel at the speed of light.

# Alien LIFE

Since humans first realized Earth wasn't the only planet in the universe, people have wondered if life exists in other parts of space. But what would aliens look like, and how would they act?

Often, we imagine alien beings as looking a little like humans. They walk on two legs and have heads on top of their bodies, with two eyes. But these ideas come from our imagination: no one has ever met an alien. That doesn't mean there is no life on other planets. In fact, the building blocks for life on Earth came from

If aliens exist, would they be friendly or hostile?

comets or meteors in space. There are more than 100 billion stars in our galaxy, many with dozens of planets—and there are hundreds of billions of galaxies.

## Long Distance

If billions upon billions of other planets exist, perhaps one of them might support a form of life. But if it exists, it's very far away. Unless we figure out how to travel faster than light, we're unlikely to meet any aliens any time soon.

## Mystery File:
### SETI PROJECT

If we can't meet aliens, maybe we can hear them. The Search for Extraterrestrial Intelligence (SETI) Project uses powerful radio telescopes to listen for signals from aliens. We've also been sending radio signals to space for 100 years.

Mystery words...

extraterrestrial: something that originates from beyond Earth

# TELEPORTATION

The hours spent waiting in line at airports and on airplanes usually feel long and boring. Just imagine if we could step into a booth in one place and arrive instantly in another place.

The word teleportation first appeared in 1931. It is a combination of Greek and Latin words and means "to carry over a distance." But the ability to travel from place to place instantly is a very old idea. The idea first appeared in traditional stories such as *The Arabian Nights* as a form of magic.

## Energy Transfer

Science fiction writers noted that energy travels at the speed of light. If we could change our bodies from matter to energy, we could send that energy millions of times faster than the fastest airplanes and turn it back into matter at the end.

Two questions remain: could we build machines to do this? And could we actually survive the process of teleportation?

## Mystery File: QUANTUM THEORY

Scientists think a key to teleportation might lie in **quantum** physics. Quantum physicists study particles that make up atoms. Some scientists think these particles might be related in ways that make it possible to move energy from place to place.

Mystery words...

**quantum:** related to particles smaller than atoms

# INVISIBILITY

At one time or another, everyone has wanted to be invisible. You could sit unseen and listen to private conversations. You could avoid getting into trouble. The military would love to get invisible soldiers deep into enemy territory to spy.

When we see things, we really see the light reflected from them. For something to be invisible, it would have to stop reflecting light. We can be fooled into thinking that things are invisible. Animals use camouflage to hide from predators. A chameleon changes the color of its skin to blend into its surroundings.

Onscreen, the Invisible Man wrapped himself in bandages to be seen.

# Mystery File:
## STEPS AHEAD

In 2012 scientists bent **microwaves** around an object making it invisible to, well, other microwaves. If scientists could learn how to bend lightwaves around objects, those objects would seem to us to disappear. It might be a way forward for camouflage.

*Invisibility would be a useful tool for a spy.*

The military uses camouflage to convince the enemy that there's no one attacking through a forest or an open field. More recently, stealth technology has been developed to hide airplanes from enemy **radar** systems.

## Bouncing Light

Scientists have yet to discover a way of stopping light from bouncing off objects and hitting our eyes. There are still no invisibility cloaks, but scientists haven't stopped trying to create them.

Mystery words...

# Thinking
# AUTOMATA

The idea of machines that can think for themselves is as old as the ancient Greeks. Since the invention of computers and **automata**, or robots, people have wondered if it will ever be possible to create a robot that thinks like a person. How different would the robot be from a real human?

Mystery words...

automata: machines built in the shape of humans

Computers are far smaller and more powerful than they used to be. Scientists have also made machines with tiny motors and complex parts. Combine these things and it's easy to imagine androids (robots) that seem to be human. Scientists have already created machines that can copy human actions.

## World of Robots

Making a robot that moves realistically is one thing.

Would a thinking robot help humans or try to conquer them?

## Mystery File:
## THE TURING TEST

In 1950, Alan Turing designed a test to see if machines could think. A human and a machine talk to a judge (who can't see them) through text messages. The machine has to convince the judge it is human. So far, no machine has passed.

Could we make a robot that is smart enough to fool humans? There are many books and movies about this idea. Some people think it would be a nightmare. They believe that these super-smart robots might try to take over the world. Other people think that robots would help us and make our lives better.

# Through a
# BLACK HOLE

Black holes are objects in space. They are so heavy and dense that not even light can escape their gravity, or pull. They're often the remains of stars that collapsed after they burned through all their fuel.

Anything that enters a black hole is crushed.

Scientists believe there is a supermassive black hole in the center of our galaxy. It is 2.5 million times heavier than the Sun.

Black holes were first described by scientists such as Albert Einstein, early in the 20th century. Black holes absorb light, so it is impossible to see them. They can only be found by seeing the effects they have on nearby stars.

## Holes in Space

Some movies depict black holes as mysterious portals, or gateways. Spacecraft might be dragged into them by their tremendous gravity and emerge in other galaxies or universes.

In fact, such holes are not black holes. They are more like wormholes, which are tunnels that are thought to connect different points in the fabric of space and time. Any matter that enters a black hole isn't going anywhere: it just gets crushed.

### Mystery File: ON THE SURFACE

Scientists study how black holes deal with the vast amounts of matter they suck in. Where does it all go to? One idea is that it gets spread all over the surface inside the black hole, which is a bit like the walls of a tunnel.

Mystery words...

dense: ethe heaviness of an object relative to its size

25

# Creating GOLD

Some early scientists were interested in more than just solving the mysteries of the universe. Some wanted to get rich quick. An easy way would be to take a worthless metal like lead and find a way to change it into gold.

This kind of early chemistry is called alchemy. It is nearly as old as civilization. In ancient times, alchemy was seen almost as a kind of magic. Alchemists believed there were secret substances on Earth that could do amazing things. In very basic workshops, they searched for substances that could change metals into gold, cure all diseases, or dissolve any material. They found nothing that worked.

Changing lead into gold has actually happened. Russian scientists did it by accident when radiation in a nuclear reactor turned the lead shielding into gold. But the energy needed to do this cost more than the gold it created.

*Alchemists in the middle ages were seen as eccentric magicians.*

## Alchemy and Modern Science

People now know that alchemy is not really a science. Its goals were impossible. But the early discoveries of alchemy led to a better understanding of real science, such as chemistry and **physics**.

The difference between alchemists and scientists is that scientists aren't looking for quick fixes. Instead, they're looking for answers and trying to improve their knowledge of the world around them.

Mystery words...

physics: the science that studies matter, energy, and forces

# The Death RAY

Many movies show aliens blasting objects and people with lasers. Aliens use death rays to destroy planets. On Earth, the military has been trying to make such weapons a reality.

A gun is too small to hold a powerful laser.

Lasers already exist. A laser is a very focused light beam that is **amplified** to make it far more powerful. A laser weapon has not yet been invented. To be powerful enough to work, the laser would be too big to fit inside a gun. But lasers have many other uses. Less powerful lasers can be used to make cuts in metal, to measure the speed of objects or how far away they are, or to point at words on a chalkboard.

## A Mad Scientist

Lasers aren't the only potential death rays. Electricity or microwaves could also do a lot of damage. In the early 20th century, physicist Nikola Tesla claimed to have designed a death ray. It would use electricity to **disable** fleets of ships. Tesla's claim helped earn him a reputation as a "mad scientist."

In the 1980s, lasers were planned to be at the heart of the U.S. Strategic Defence Initiative, also called "Star Wars." Lasers would be placed in space to shoot down incoming missiles. The technology proved too complicated and expensive.

Mystery words...

disable: to cause not to work

# Glossary

**accelerating** moving increasingly faster

**amplified** Made louder or stronger

**automata** Machines built in the shape of humans

**cells** Microscopic divisions of living matter within the body

**dense** Describing the heaviness of an object relative to its size; very dense objects are heavy but small

**disable** To cause not to work

**eternal** Something that lasts forever

**extraterrestrial** Something that originates from beyond Earth

**friction** The resistance created when objects rub together

**gene** The part of a cell that tells it how to live and grow

**genetic** Related to genes, which control the growth of the body

**gravity** The force that attracts objects toward one another

**inorganic** Matter that is not alive, such as rocks

**lubricants** Substances such as oil that make surfaces slip easily past each other

**microwaves** Waves of energy with a very short wavelength

**perpetual** Going on forever

**philosopher** Someone who studies the nature of reality

**physics** The science that studies matter, energy, and forces

**quantum** Related to particles smaller than atoms

**radar** A system that uses radio signals to detect objects

**satellites** Objects that orbit around a planet

**science fiction** Stories based on future technology and science

# Find Out More

## BOOKS

Bailey, Diane. *The Future of Space Exploration* (What's Next?). Creative Education, 2012.

Ditmer, Lori. *The Future of Medicine* (What's Next?). Creative Education, 2012.

Halls, Kelly Milner. *Alien Investigation: Searching for the Truth About UFOs and Aliens*. Millbrook Press, 2012.

Jacobson, Ryan. *How Lasers Work* (Discovering How Things Work). Child's World, 2011.

Rau, Dana Meachen. *Robots* (Bookworms; Surprising Science). Benchmark Books, 2010.

## WEBSITES

Discovery Kids Science
*http://kids.discovery.com/tell-me/science*

Science for Kids
*www.sciencekids.co.nz*

Science News for Kids
*www.sciencenewsforkids.org*

Bill Nye the Science Guy
*www.billnye.com*

The Exploratorium
*www.exploratorium.edu*

# Index